Some

Logical Arguments

Against

Premarital Sex

Published by: Peter Ananti-Tetteh Jnr.

ISBN: 978-9988-1-6651-9

For all enquiries contact:
Peter Ananti-Tetteh Jnr.

P. O. Box KA 30480 Kotoka International Airport
Accra - Ghana
West Africa

Tel: +233 (0) 205421993 / +233 (0) 544710198
+233 (0) 266036352

Table of Content

PREFACE

Human beings have been in search of freedom since time immemorial. If our freedom becomes absolute, the desires of the flesh control us and lead us astray. Indeed, not everything that the flesh desires is good for it. **It is all right to be tempted, but it is all wrong to yield to temptation.** GOD has given us the ability to overcome temptation whenever it confronts us. 1 Cor. 10:13 assures us that HE will not allow us to be tempted beyond what we can bear. The stress test of abstinence is one that we must and can pass.

Humans are the most important of God's creation.

Sex is the natural process or activity that leads to the formation of a human being in the womb. It is a sacred or holy act and must be treated with respect. We must endeavour to abstain till we enter into the holy union of marriage.

PETER ANANTI-TETTEH JNR.

ACKNOWLEDGEMENT

I would like to thank the following for helping to ensure the publication of this book:

My parents, Evangelist Peter Ananti-Tetteh and Mrs. Christine Ananti-Tetteh; and my brothers, David Ananti-Tetteh and Dieudonné Ananti-Tetteh, for their support in diverse ways.

I would also like to thank the following Christian brothers and sisters for their help in more ways than one.

Mr Emmanuel Asare, Mr. Joseph Opata Williams, Mr. John Teye-Wayo Kuwornu, Mrs. Reeta Auguste all of the Ring Road Church of Christ, Mrs. Zenabu Mensah of the Osu Church of Christ, Mr. Eric Ofori-Gyan of the Kwabenya Church of Christ, Evangelist Michael Ghartey of the La Church of Christ and Evangelist George Abugah of the Legon Church of Christ.

I am also grateful to Mrs. Sarah Nelson (the patron for the youth of the Ring Road Church of Christ), and the youth of the Ring Road Church of Christ for their encouragement and critical questions. I also acknowledge the support and prayers of the membership of the Ring Road Church of Christ.

I also thank all others who contributed to the success of this book on my blind side. Certainly GOD has seen your good works and will surely bless you.

Above all I thank GOD immensely for crowning my efforts with success.

DEDICATION
This book is dedicated to the **Ring Road Church of Christ.**

SOME LOGICAL ARGUMENTS AGAINST PREMARITAL SEX

15 Relevant Quotes By Peter Ananti-Tetteh Jnr (The Author)

1. Any advantage of premarital sex is an advantage with a baggage.

2. You must love your marriage well enough to reserve all the intimate moments for it.

3. The greater the difference between your marriage and your courtship the more excited you will be about your marriage.

4. The longer the period of denial, the higher the level of sensation.

5. The accumulated stress, when released at the appropriate time, produces desirable results.

6. Hot-Blooded Passion + Stress or Pressure = Explosion of passion.

7. The highest passion produces the lowest tension.

8. At any rate, the passion is not enough for the full length of a long- lasting marriage.

9. Your marriage desperately needs all the passion you can give to it.

10. The passion is too strong to last for long.

11. You cannot prevent the passion from finishing, but you can delay the finishing point of the passion.

12. Indulging in premarital sex is like taking part in an 800 metre race just before a 10 kilometre marathon.

13. Engaging in premarital sex is like playing the opening match before the opening ceremony.

14. Premarital sex can never qualify as a curtain raiser to marriage.

15 It is all right to be tempted, but it is all wrong to yield to temptation.

CHAPTER 1

INTRODUCTION

There is too much buzz around sex; there is too much hype around sex (sex is overrated, sex is over hyped); and thus sex has been greatly cheapened. It has been observed that in many societies love is gradually losing its status to sex. There is a more than necessary focus on sex. Many newspapers, movies, adverts, music videos, songs, paintings, pictures billboards etc. clearly reveal this. The advisability or otherwise of premarital sex has actually been an age old debate. Premarital sex has been a problem for generations but it is more pronounced in our time because of the buzz around sex in sections of the media. Censorship is weak. Today's youth is like an amateur boxer without a protective headgear (the boxing head guard). And so the youth are "receiving punches directly to their heads." The youth need extra protection compared to the older population. Only Adam and Eve did not face the challenge of premarital sex since Eve was presented to Adam by God as his wife right from the very onset. Adam and eve became husband and wife on the very first day they met. In fact soon after they met. God performed the marriage ceremony just as he presented Eve to Adam.

The issue of premarital sex will therefore be relevant always since Adam and Eve's unique situation will not recur anywhere in the world.

The buzz around sex has raised the expectations about sex so high that people cannot meet these expectations, like the bar of a high jump that has been raised too high that you cannot jump over it. It has to be lowered. In this case, the bar of expectations represents the expectations of pleasure obtained from sex. Many people engage in pleasure seeking adventures by sleeping around but they never experience the level of pleasure they are looking for. They look for extraordinary pleasure from sex so they are never content. No matter how many people they sleep with they are never satisfied. They never get enough. The more they sleep with people the more they are dissatisfied. Eccl 5:10a says that he that loveth silver shall not be satisfied with silver. Similarly he that loveth sex shall not be satisfied with sex. Worldly pleasures do not give us permanent satisfaction. Economists say that man's needs are insatiable. If man's needs are insatiable, how much more his wants? Changing sexual partners is not a need--It is a want!

People who lead sexually promiscuous lifestyles are chasing worldly pleasures and they obtain temporary satisfaction from them. The satisfaction obtained dies down quickly i.e. they keep on getting back to square one (1).

Yet they keep on chasing these pleasures. It is a pathetic cycle. People who sleep with many people have unrealistic expectations about sex. Indeed if one has realistic expectations of pleasure from sex, one will stick to just one (1) partner (that is, one's husband or wife). One person can satisfy your basic sexual needs.

Some sports journalists overhype matches thereby raising expectations to unrealistic levels. They raise the hopes of soccer fans so high that the matches eventually do not live up to expectations. We must lower our expectations about sex to realistic levels. We must manage our expectations about sex so that we are not disappointed in the end.

People who sleep with many people are breaking a lot of hearts. This is because emotions and hearts are involved in sex. Some claim their emotions don't get in the way, but some way or somehow their emotions get involved.

These include positive and negative emotions like joy, satisfaction, regret or revenge depending on the circumstances surrounding the sexual act. The negative emotions are usually associated with issues like rape or a person trying to infect someone with an STD like AIDS, as pay back for a hurtful deed. People who sell their bodies often experience a feeling of self pity and depression (a strong feeling of a lack of self worth and of being dirty). We can't completely detach emotions from sex; sex and emotions cannot be totally decoupled.

Agape love is so great that it can be shared by billions of people (with leftovers) but Romantic love is so small that it can be shared by just two (2) people. Sex is too intimate an activity to take for granted, to joke with or to engage in with just anybody. It is not child's play. Sex is not for children or teenagers. It is for mature people. It should not happen by chance or on the spur of the moment between two people who are not married to each other. Meaning that one-night- stands are completely unacceptable. One-night-stand is casual sex and it is wrong.

One should not rush into sex. It is said that, "If you rush you will crash!" There is more to sex than meets the eye. Sex is not a joke, it is serious business. It has to be engaged in with someone you consider to be the most special person to you. Only one individual can occupy the position of "most special person" A promiscuous person cannot consider everyone he or she sleeps with as the most special person in his or her life. If you sleep with someone and he or she gets to know that you later on slept with someone else, the previous person you slept with is likely to feel used, disrespected, inadequate or simply not good enough.

This (previous) person will then realize that he or she was not the most special person to you all along, even though before you had sex you said sweet words to him or her and made him or her feel so dear to you.

The practice of sowing one's wild oats (i.e. embarking on irresponsible pleasure seeking adventures) before one gets married is very costly. One may have a number of illegitimate children with different mothers or fathers. There may be a resultant broken home. Family life is then destroyed. The children will be greatly affected, deadly diseases could be contracted. People who live promiscuous lives also live complicated lives. Their lives are ultimately involved in the lives of many people in delicate ways. When you make any sexual contact with a person, you get directly or remotely involved in the

[4]

life of that person for as long as you can imagine. You can't avoid it. Promiscuous people keep on lying and avoiding people in order to ensure that they are not found out. Having two lovers is having one too many.

Many people have very wrong conceptions about sex. For instance some men demand sex from women as evidence of the women's love for them.

It is established that sex is for mutual satisfaction and not self gratification. The term verbal intercourse refers to an interaction, dialogue or chat. The sexual act is a kind of interaction hence the word sexual intercourse. We don't interact or chat with somebody by force. Both people participate willingly in a dialogue. No one should be pressurized into sex. The demand for sex is not in harmony with the idea of being gentle.

(The two underlined above, are on opposite sides). And for any lady in a relationship, if after copious advice the man insists on premarital sex without backing down, let him go. On the other hand psychologists observe that some women are of the opinion that they need approval from the men they sleep with to confirm that they are ready for marriage. Paul Popenoe in his book, "Are Virgins out of date" asserts that this creates anxiety and a mentality of failure if such women don't receive this approval from the men they sleep with. Again he observes that if many men pressurize a particular woman into sex, it does not mean that she is popular. It only suggests that those men are being lustful.

Every human being consists of a body, soul and spirit. Sex involves a connection between two bodies, two souls and two spirits. It is not a mere physical activity or connection. It is also a spiritual connection.

Sexual sins therefore, have spiritual implications. Sexual sins make you spiritually weak. The Devil can "get you" or destroy you easily because you lose GOD's protection. "Bullets" fired at you by the Devil can hit and kill you because you are spiritually vulnerable. There is a tendency to dismiss spiritual issues as mythical. But a spiritual realm does exist! If a spiritual realm does not exist it means God does not exist, because GOD is a spirit.

GOD heads the spiritual realm. So when you avoid sexual sins HE protects you from spiritual wickedness in high places (Eph. 6:12 and subsequent verses of the chapter). Science is limited to the physical realm. Witchcraft on display and other spiritual phenomena cannot be explained by scientific theories, formulae and experiments (and these include natural, physical and social sciences). Even atheists agree that there are certain happenings that can never ever be explained by scientific principles. These are spiritual events!

It is very clear that we cannot overlook all these dimensions to sex. We must have the right conception about sex if we are to understand it.

CHAPTER 2

SOME MISCONCEPTIONS ABOUT PREMARITAL SEX AND THEIR COUNTER ARGUMENTS

A) Misconception: You must have experience in having sex before you get married, in order to have a successful marriage.

Counter Argument: It is not experience in having sex that ensures a successful marriage but commitment. If it's experience (in having sex) that you are looking for, you will get that experience definitely when you finally get married. Those who engage in premarital sex have experience in having sex and those who remain as virgins till they get married, have experience in **abstaining from sex**. This experience in abstaining from sex will help you in marriage. This is because even in marriage, there are situations that demand abstinence. For instance when your partner is sick or has travelled. In such situations it will be relatively easier for you to abstain. The period from the time you become sexually aware till you get married is a critical period which should be used for the mastering of the art of abstinence. The moment you become sexually aware you must start abstaining. You must ensure that you are already a graduate of abstinence, before you marry. Joseph was a graduate of abstinence. (Genesis 39:6-21) You must have mastered the art of abstinence before saying I do! Mastery of the art of abstinence is a pre-requisite or a pre-requirement for marriage (it is part of the marriage checklist). A husband and a wife who abstained from pre-marital sex will trust each other to be sexually faithful in the marriage even when they are separated by distance for years due to demands of work etc. You may be experienced in having sex but may not have self control and this will ruin your marriage **.You must rather have experience in abstaining from sex in**

order to have a successful marriage. It is disastrous to enter into marriage with little or no experience in abstinence. *IF YOU ARE NOT YET MARRIED, DO NOT MISS THIS GOD GIVEN OPPORTUNITY TO LEARN OR TEACH YOURSELF HOW TO ABSTAIN FROM SEX.*

B)   Misconception: Not everyone can abstain.

Counter Argument: Everyone has the capacity to abstain. The problem however is that, some people do not develop the capacity. The capacity must be developed. To develop this capacity, take a firm decision to abstain, make a conscious effort to abstain from day to day, pray about it and seek Christian counselling or psychological help if necessary. Before you know it, you would have mastered the art of abstinence. Some maintain that the sexual urge is so compelling that you cannot help it. It is false! You can and must control it. Yes, the sexual urge is powerful but what is power without control? Power without control will lead to disaster. If you truly make up your mind to abstain, you will be able to abstain. It is said that the decision to abstain is half the battle won. We are too fond of underrating ourselves. Oh! I can't do this, no! I can't do that, meanwhile the potential exist! If your capacity to abstain is just 1 day, you can upgrade to 1 month. Then you immediately upgrade it to 3 months. Then make 6 months your target. If you keep on upgrading your capacity, you will end up abstaining for years. It is a widely known fact that we do not graduate from our self improvement programmes. The room for improvement is always roomy. Therefore you can keep on upgrading your abstinence capacity without end or without limits.

C)   Misconception: Abstinence is Ideal but not Real.

Counter Argument: Abstinence is Ideal and Real. (i) Ideal because you save yourself from a lot of trouble or complications such as unwanted pregnancies and sexually transmitted diseases, when you abstain. Besides your conscience is clear when you abstain from pre-marital sex. (ii) And <u>Real</u> because people are doing it (i.e. people are abstaining). It can be done!!!

D)   Misconception: Everybody is doing it.

Counter Argument: This is not true! (It is pure propaganda). In 1Kings 19: verse 10 and 18, Elijah the prophet thought everybody worshiped Baal, but GOD told Elijah that 7000 people in Israel did not worship Baal. Anyone who says everybody is doing it, is certainly not everybody's spokesman. There are still youth in today's world who believe in the sanctity of sex. There are still some young men and women who are abstaining from premarital sex. They however do not announce it since it is a private affair. Besides, not everyman will demand sex during courtship. These men are too decent to demand sex. They are able to fight back their sexual feelings and with the same attitude they can "fight" to protect their marriages. *"No True Gentleman Demands Sex"*. One can still find gentlemen who will help a lady in distress without seeking any favour from her.

You can't demand sex and still be a gentleman. Love is unconditional. You should not demand sex for love. The expression of love is not limited to sex. There are a thousand and one ways of expressing love. The BIBLE tells us that love is patient. And so if a man loves a woman he should be able to wait. If you learn how to abstain from premarital sex (fornication) it will be easier for you to abstain from extramarital sex (adultery).

E)   Misconception: Premarital sex is part of sex education.

Counter Argument: Education consists of (a) theory and (b) practical(s). So when it comes to sex education you do the theory before marriage and do the practical(s) when you get married. If you are not yet married stick to the THEORY!—(No practical(s) for you). You are supposed to serve a ban on sex if you are not married. The ban on sex ends or is lifted when you get married.

F)   Misconception: Abstinence is not good for your mental hygiene. You will develop psychological or emotional problems if you abstain from sex till marriage.

Counter Argument: Abstinence means self control and it's a sign of maturity. There are natural urges in the body which must be suppressed until the appropriate time arrives for each of these urges to be expressed. For instance the urge to urinate must be suppressed till the time and place are appropriate. A child who does not urinate in bed but suppresses the urine till he or she gets to a urinal is obviously mature. It is for the sake of the health of that child that he or she controls the bladder. The act of controlling the urge to urinate or the urge to have sex is scientifically known as ***continence***. It is a healthy practice. Continence is biologically or medically acceptable. You can be psychologically or emotionally stable even when you abstain from sex. When you abstain it does not mean you are repressed it means you are highly disciplined. Abstinence will not affect the way you interact or socialize with the opposite sex. According to psychologists, early sex can result in arrested emotional maturity in teenagers.

G)   Misconception: Many years of abstinence will make you infertile. "If you don't use it, you will lose it."

Counter Argument: Abstinence does not interfere with the normal functions of the reproductive system. A woman's reproductive cycle does not cease because of abstinence. A man experiences nocturnal emissions, which engage the reproductive system and ensure that the mechanism involved does not fail. Health experts report that abstinence has also got health benefits. Certain essential substances are conserved in the body when you abstain.

H)   Misconception: Virginity is not important. Most men don't like virgins anyway.

Counter Argument: Virgins are highly ranked by men. About 90% of men prefer to marry virgins. We are quiet familiar with the words of this Hip-Life song by Reggie Zippy "Bɛɛma biara sɔre a ɔpɛ Virgin na wayɛ nu wedding..." Men regard women who keep their virginity till marriage as independent minded and focused. It is incorrect to say that virginity is merely something to get rid of. "An unmarried woman's dignity is in her virginity" so says an African proverb. Now, virginity is not a feminine term. Men should also commit to remaining as virgins till they get married. A typical customer will not like to buy a product with a broken seal. Do not break your virginity before marriage.

I)   Misconception: If you enter into marriage as a virgin you will be embarrassed because of the inexperience in having sex.

Counter Argument: Scenario (i) Do you prefer to be embarrassed in the presence of someone who is not married to you and who is very likely to tell other people about what happened and ridicule you with his or her friends? He or she will have access to private or confidential or sensitive information about you because of the sexual encounter between the two of you and may blackmail you because he or she is not married to you.

Scenario (ii) However, if you get embarrassed in marriage, your husband or wife is very likely to protect your privacy since your disgrace is his or her disgrace. Husbands and wives are in binding relationships. They share secrets and confide in each

[11]

other. They have made special vows to each other in the presence of witnesses. If there will be any embarrassment at all, it will occur either in scenario (i) or scenario (ii). There is no other scenario. Scenario (ii) is obviously better.

The fact that you must abstain from sex till marriage does not mean you should be naive about sex. You can obtain good sex education by reading medical literature or Christian books about marriage. Avoid learning about sex from vulgar or pornographic or profane sources. Seek Christian premarital counselling and you can make the necessary sexual adjustment in marriage. Post-marital counseling is also advisable. Sexuality is an instinct; your instincts will guide you. (Therefore you don't need experience in having sex before you get married). An instinct is a natural ability you are born with. Our instincts develop with time and get to their best levels when we are mature. When a child is born he or she is able to suck the breast minutes after delivery without being taught how to do so by his or her mother. This is because it is an instinctive act. The belief in GOD is an instinct. Atheist ignore this instinct within them. Obi nkyerɛ akwadaa NYAME" is a Twi proverb which means that nobody makes a child aware of the existence of GOD. The child gets to know about the existence of GOD instinctively. In the world of wildlife a lion teaches its cub how to hunt for food and defend itself against enemies, but not how to mate. Nevertheless when the young lion grows, it knows what to do. (Some people argue that (i) How can you drive a car successfully without learning how to drive first?

(ii) How can a man go hunting if he has never fired a gun before?)
Driving and hunting etc. are not instincts. You therefore need training before embarking on these activities. Since sexuality is an instinct you need no training in having sex before you get married. If you need any training at all, it is training in the skill of abstinence. You can learn valuable lessons in impulse control.

[12]

J)   Misconception: You must engage in premarital sex to find out whether the two of you are sexually compatible or are capable of having children.

Counter Argument: To find out if you are fertile or sexually compatible, visit a fertility clinic or hospital in order to be examined by a specialist like a urologist (for men) or gynaecologist (for women). The specialists will thoroughly examine your reproductive systems and advise you appropriately. Before one embarks on a long journey (a journey abroad or a journey of many miles) a medical examination is usually conducted. Now marriage is a long journey of many years. Shouldn't you undergo a thorough medical examination before embarking on such a long journey? It is commonly argued that "How can you buy a car without taking a test drive?" and "You must test the waters before you dive into the river in order to know its temperature and depth." I agree there has to be a test but "let the doctors do the testing". They will screen you well. The test you will conduct comes nowhere near what a specialist doctor will conduct on you and your partner. Even doctors need to be examined by other doctors (third parties) in order to obtain independent or unbiased assessments. If the medical examination reveals that you are not compatible, you can part company without anyone feeling exploited. However, if a person sleeps with you, and you find out that the two of you are not compatible, it means that you have been exploited and dumped. Indeed, people can take advantage of you under the pretext of testing. There are people who will always test but will never buy. If you sleep with someone and you become convinced that the two of you are compatible, you will have cleared the doubt but then you will have robbed your marriage of the full dose of passion it needs.

K)   Misconception: Do it just once and then wait till

marriage.

Counter Argument: As the saying goes, "Once you start you can't stop" (at least for most people). It is like walking down the steep side of a hill under the force of gravity. It is very difficult to stand still even if one so wishes. In this case the inhibitions of the individual have been broken. From the scientific point of view, the body has been sexually awakened even though he or she has not yet mastered the art of abstinence. He or she can get addicted. Besides, sex before marriage is a sin (and it doesn't matter whether it is protected sex or unprotected sex). If you have mastered the art of abstinence, addiction will not be a problem.

L)   Misconception: Sex before marriage will solidify the relationship and will increase the chances of the two of you getting married to each other.

Counter Argument: Only a small percentage of such relationships will actually end up in marriage simply because they had sex. Usually they get married because of other reasons or considerations. In fact, sex before marriage increases the chances of a break up. This is because the two individuals have already experienced the highest level of intimacy (i.e. sex). There is no other activity that is more intimate than sex. Therefore if they break up they will not miss or lose anything. They can afford not to marry each other. They may be following this common principle, "Why buy the whole cow when you can get the milk for free? It is therefore not safe to say that "since we have promised to marry each other we can go ahead and have sex."

M)   Misconception: Variety is the spice of life therefore you can have affairs (sex) with as many people as possible before marriage. (You must sow your wild oats before marriage because it is your only chance to do so).

Counter Argument: Variety is indeed the spice of life but it does not apply in every case. You cannot argue that variety is the spice of life therefore you will be a Christian for one month, a Moslem for another month, a Buddhist for another month and a Hindu for another month. You cannot cope with the different rules and regulations (a lot of them are opposite to each other). If you have multiple sexual partners before marriage you will become used to variety. If you finally get married you will have to stick to your wife or husband (that is monotony). And you will be making unnecessary comparisons between previous sexual partners and your husband or wife. It will be very difficult to make a transition from variety to monotony unless God intervenes. Do not deliberately get yourself into this problem so that you can ask for God's intervention. Prevention is better than cure. Must we continue in sin so that grace may abound? Romans 6:1.

N)   Misconception: When we preach abstinence we deprive people of one of their natural rights.

Counter Argument: A right must be exercised at the right time. A person may have the right to hunt for animals in the forest but cannot hunt before or beyond the hunting season. Sex before or outside of marriage is wrong.

CHAPTER 3

PREMARITAL SEX AND MARITAL SEX CONTRASTED

The sexual act should not be toyed with because through sex you obtain access to classified information about the other person and the other person also obtains classified information about you. Not just anyone should have access to this private, sensitive or classified information about you. In the security services people take vows or (oaths) before they are exposed to or given access to classified (private) or sensitive information. A man and a woman must take special vows at a marriage ceremony in the presence of others before they have access to this classified information through sex. Sex must take place between two people who have made special vows to each other. Sex is exclusive to marriage. You must belong to an institution before you have access to classified information about that institution. Similarly you must belong to the institution of marriage before you gain access to the classified information obtained through sex. Security agencies need warrants to inquire about private information (A search warrant is an example). Sex is an inquiry into a person's personality. And you need a warrant to conduct this inquiry. Your marriage certificate or anything that attests to the fact that you are married, is the warrant you need.

Paul Popenoe writes that during **marital sex** (in a healthy marriage), there is a complete surrender of each one to the other i.e. you give yourselves to each other (husband and wife lower their defences around themselves). You don't hold back. You truly let go. You freely express your sexual feelings. Sigmund Freud observes that your whole personality goes with it. This is because you are not doubtful or double-minded. Your conscience is clear. There is no psychological or mental torture. There is absolutely no feeling of guilt. When sex occurs in marriage there is emotional security since the relationship is a legally binding one.

And in the right atmosphere you will be physiologically prepared. Your brain will be at ease and it will ensure that the heart pumps the right amount of blood to the right areas. The right amount of chemicals, hormones and fluids will be released. The relevant body organs function at their optimum levels. Marital sex is spiritually all right. It receives the blessings of GOD.

Your soul "feels good" because you are at peace with yourself. The therapeutic effect of sex is actually realized in marriage. The bottom line is that for sex to be worth your while you must be emotionally, physically and physiologically prepared before engaging in the act and this is ensured in a healthy marriage.

You are likely to find this inscription on most beverages, "Best served chilled". In the same way, sex is best served in marriage. (For the best results sex must take place in the holy union of marriage). The bare fact is that marital sex has got so many advantages over premarital sex.

In sharp contrast, a lot of anxiety is associated with **premarital sex** because of the fear of getting caught or being found out. There is also the fear of pregnancy and of contracting diseases. Your privacy may be greatly compromised since your illegitimate partner can breach your trust by telling other people exactly what you did in secret.

There is a feeling of guilt because it is a sin. This load of guilt mars the pleasure after a short period. And there is a great chance of one suffering from psychological torture because of the pricking of one's conscience. There is no emotional security because you are not in a legally binding relationship and you are not sure whether he or she is using you or not. Again this doubt about the intentions of the other party soon overshadows whatever enjoyment you seek for. He or she can just break up with you or walk out of the relationship at any time and with ease because there is no commitment. On the other hand divorce or separation in marriage involves a long or tough legal process. Both extended families can even intervene to save the marriage. A break up is not easy. In premarital sex there is an obvious likelihood of one or both partners holding back as a result of doubt about the commitment of the other partner. If you give your all and he or she breaks up with you, the heart-break will be massive. There is no complete surrender. This psychological state hampers the physiological preparation of the body. The brain is therefore not at ease (it becomes tensed) and so it does not ensure that the heart pumps the right amount of blood to the relevant areas of the body. Also the brain does not cause the release of the right amount of chemicals, hormones and fluids. It means that you are shortchanged in the act of premarital sex. The pleasure is below standard (below the optimum level). Why settle for less? Premarital sex causes spiritual damage to the individual. Advocates of premarital sex argue that abstinence is anti-enjoyment and that we must be allowed to enjoy ourselves. The counter argument to this statement is this, "if it is enjoyment you are looking for then you may as well go for maximum enjoyment (which is only achievable in marriage). Marital sex is original, premarital sex is an imitation. Choose the original. The negatives of premarital sex are also associated with extramarital sex.

It is helpful for a prospective couple to discuss controversial and confidential issues such as topics relating to sex, during the latter stages of courtship when it is certain that the relationship will lead to marriage. These discussions should be held specifically at the period when premarital counselling is going on. They must have a thorough and objective discussion about sex (not graphic) in order to avoid rude shocks later on in marriage. Some married men and women are promiscuous because they usually have poor communication about sex with their spouses. Sex should not be treated as a taboo topic by the prospective couple.

But a man and woman in courtship must:
:

(1) avoid getting into dark, secluded or deserted places,
(2) avoid pornographic materials since they corrupt the mind,
(3) avoid petting or fondling, for it speeds up the arousal process.

Petting is therefore a catalyst to arousal. Arousal prepares the body for sex and there is no point preparing your body for sex in the courtship period when you must avoid sex before marriage. These three examples increase the risk of fornication or premarital sex.

CHAPTER 4

AROUSAL MANAGEMENT AND THE NEED FOR IT

Most men (not all men) are in the habit of pressuring women into sex. There are quiet a number of reasons why it is so. These reasons or factors include, (1) men are stimulated visually and the visual stimulus is very powerful. Visual stimuli send a lot of information across to the recipient. For instance you can determine the height, size, colour and sometimes texture of something by simply looking at it. Visual teaching aids therefore make very effective learning. Jesus' miracles could be seen by the people and it convinced them to follow Him.(2) Arousal is very quick in men (sometimes it takes just a few seconds). On the contrary, arousal is slow in women .
For a man, arousal is virtually a daily affair.

(3)Men are traditionally empowered to propose to women. Men are therefore encouraged or socialized to make the first move in various aspects of life. Men are natural initiative takers (that is their strength) and women are natural care givers (that is also their strength). It however does not mean that men cannot give care nor does it mean that women cannot take initiatives.

(4)The male hormone (testosterone) is an aggressive hormone, hence the aggressive nature of most men. Testosterone emboldens men and makes it relatively easier for them to break through the fear barrier. Suicide statistics show that even though more women attempt suicide than men, more men are able to commit suicide than women. The numerous women who contemplate suicide lack the nerve or drive to put it into action. Only a few women do. Boys generally partake in more aggressive or risky sporting activities compared to girls. And the boys grow into men with this aggressiveness.

Testosterone is also responsible for the sex drive and testosterone makes a man who he is. Men have a lot of testosterone whiles women have low amounts of testosterone.

Consequently men are more likely to make sexual advances at women. (Nevertheless men can exercise self control if they so decide). Arousal is an involuntary action and this is so for both males and females.

Even though arousal is an involuntary action, you can prevent arousal by avoiding sexually explicit images and literature in the media and elsewhere. The "push" factors listed above individually and collectively constitute a powerful force. These combined factors sum up the woes of many a man (just one of the factors is troublesome enough) but the fact that you are pushed does not mean you should move. One frustrated lady once said "it is not my fault that I am beautiful, it is not my fault that I am attractive." She is right, it is not her fault!

It is not a man's fault that he is easily aroused (that is how GOD made him), but it is his fault if he commits a sexual sin because he is aroused.

Every virile man undergoes a strong internal struggle with respect to arousal. The quick arousal of a man is a challenge he must overcome, a struggle he must win, a test of his manliness and a cross he must carry.

GOD has given men a lot of physical strength and influence in society and so he has placed this hurdle in front of men to provide balance. It is GOD's way of ensuring balance of power between men and women. A strong man is not the man who has powerful muscles but the man who can control his sexual feelings. Strong men have the energy or the velocity to flee from fornication or adultery. Samson was floored by Delilah even though he could single handedly kill hundreds of men. Samson was later on able to pull down a whole building with strength provided him by GOD. Many great men have fallen or failed to scale the hurdle because of the lack of self control. GOD has given every man the ability to scale the hurdle but most people do not pray over it or seek counseling to enhance this ability. Women have their troubles too. Being a man comes at a cost and it is the same with being a woman.

The journey to HEAVEN is a tough one full of temptations, tests or examinations. The hurdles are to ensure that we are ready for HEAVEN. When we get to HEAVEN we can then say that we have fought a good fight. (II Timothy 4:7) the crown of life will not be given to us on a silver platter. It won't come easy. Acts 14:22 tells us that we must through much tribulation enter the Kingdom of GOD. The body has its own desires, likewise the soul. Usually the desires of the body and the soul are opposite to each other. The body competes with the soul and the soul must win! In a few cases though, the desires of the soul and the body are the same. For instance the soul appreciates good, decent music hence the saying "If music is food for the soul, then play on". And the body also appreciates good, decent music.

Since arousal occurs virtually on a daily basis for men in particular, it is dangerous to express it anytime you feel it. We have many rape and defilement cases in society because the perpetrators involved are just expressing it when they feel it. It is never true that the sex impulse is a powerful drive that must not be thwarted, restrained or restricted. Paul Popenoe firmly stresses this point. He adds that expressing our sexual desires anytime we feel it reduces us to infants who want what they want, when they want it. He also makes the point that anger is another powerful impulse which when expressed anytime we feel it could lead to physical assault (or even murder).

The fact that arousal in men is triggered by visual stimulus means that it is important for a woman to always dress decently especially during courtship. This is because indecent or provocative dressing can arouse the man, and if he is not strong-minded he will pressurize the woman into premarital sex. Provocative dressing of women put ideas into the heads of men.

Provocative dressing increases the chances of women getting sexually harassed. It must however be clarified, that it doesn't mean that sexual harassment in such a case is justified. Sexual harassment can never be justified under any circumstance.

The police always advise citizens to hide their kitchen knives so that unarmed thieves who break into houses will not have access to the kitchen knives to stab occupants of each house in question. Leaving a kitchen knife lying about increases the probability of a person getting stabbed. Similarly dressing indecently increases the probability of a woman falling victim to sexual harassment or rape. It is about the probability of the unfortunate event occurring and not the justification of the unfortunate event. Some writers observe that if a man who lacks self-control goes to town and he gets aroused by an indecently dressed woman, and he does not have access to the woman, he may come back home and pounce on an innocent girl in his vicinity.

Men who sexually molest women do so for three main reasons.

1. A psychological problem, as in the case of those who defile babies or toddlers who are decently dressed or are not sexually attractive.

2. Arousal due to the indecent or provocative dressing of a woman.

3. Arousal due to exposure to pornographic materials.

If women and girls dress decently, sexual molestation due to the second reason (provocative dressing) will be eliminated, leaving behind the first reason (psychological problems) and the third reason (exposure to pornography). Even though decent dressing will not eliminate sexual molestation completely, it will significantly reduce it and that is good news. Prostitutes expose certain parts of their bodies (the breasts, thighs, etc), wear tight fitting, revealing or seductive clothes in order to arouse men (their clients) so that they will patronize their illicit services. The negative impact of indecent dressing is real and cannot be over emphasized.

Indecent dressing sends across a message or a signal of promiscuity even though it may not be intended by the people wearing the indecent clothes.

Every society has its own standard of decency but there has to be a general or universal standard to avoid chaos or confusion and to ensure orderliness. In science we have S.I. units which are universally accepted. If there is any individual or society that says that exposure of sensitive parts of the body is decent, then that individual or society has a twisted definition or a corrupted conception of decency. Both men and women have to dress decently. Indecent exposure is against the law and it is punishable. We don't have the freedom to wear just anything in public. Some women do argue that:

1. "It is my body and I feel like showing off flesh or flaunting what I have. I must accentuate my feminine features."
   Decent men find this way of dressing very disturbing. Indeed, if a decent man is interested in a woman and later on that woman dresses indecently, his respect for and interest in the woman take a nose dive (they fall sharply).

2. "I am wearing it because it is hot".
   Hot means sexually attractive. So a woman who wears "hot clothes" should not be surprised if she is sexually harassed by unscrupulous men.

3. "If you can't stand my dressing, turn your head away."
   That man has the right to look in any direction he so wishes. But in this case he will have to avoid looking in the direction of the woman so that he doesn't get aroused. His freedom to look around with ease is therefore undermined. Indecent dressing is passive sexual harassment. Okomfo Kwadee's song with the words "wo taataa me" expatiates on this issue.

There is always the need to kill the arousal whiles you are not yet married. You have to kill the arousal today for the sake of your marriage tomorrow. One preacher humorously stated that you must "kill" yourself today so that you can "resurrect" tomorrow. You don't have to satisfy the arousal.

Nobody is aroused 24 hours a day, every moment of the week. No matter the extent to which you are aroused, the arousal will eventually die down. It is commonly known that if a person is aroused and he or she receives a very shocking or disturbing news, the arousal quickly goes away.

You should therefore not be worried when you are aroused because the arousal will literally take care of itself. The process of arousal is like a roller coaster ride; when the arousal gets to its peak it then begins to drop till it gets to zero. Then you feel like you were never aroused. It is a cycle of ups and downs. Tension is created in the body when you are aroused, but when the arousal goes away the tension goes away with it. It is not true that if you don't satisfy the arousal you will become permanently tensed, dull or inactive (lethargic). Arousal is not exactly like the hunger we feel for food. When you are hungry and you do not eat any food, the hunger will never go away. In other words hunger is permanent until it is satisfied by eating. But arousal is not permanent (even if it is not satisfied). You can help it. If you do not eat or drink for many weeks you will certainly die but if you don't have sex for many years you will not die as a result. Satisfaction of arousal is an immediate want, not an immediate need.

There is no reason why a person should masturbate to obtain sexual satisfaction when he or she is aroused. It can have serious psychological and physiological effects on the individual. Masturbation is also known as solitary sex (sex involving one person) and in marriage, a person who masturbates, may prefer it to intimacy with his or her spouse. Sexual feelings are to be shared by a husband and a wife. The solo affair is a selfish one.

Ways of subduing arousal include

1. Reading a decent book that will take your mind away from the arousal.
2. Engaging in recreational or sporting activities and physical exercise like aerobics.
3. Watching wholesome entertainment programmes.
   These activities constitute a coping strategy or a stress management strategy.

There are many experts who can help people out when it comes to dealing with arousal. Suppressing your arousal is a sacrifice you must make while you are still single, since you will reap the benefits of that sacrifice in marriage.

CHAPTER 5

SOME ANALOGIES IN SUPPORT OF ABSTINENCE

"Hard on the training ground, easy on the battle field" is a fairly known saying which is relevant to the preparation for marriage. The training ground for marriage is single life. So the single life must be used for enduring the strain of abstinence. In marriage you can then be able to deal with this strain easily. Marriage is not all milk and honey. It is a virtual battlefield. Couples strive hard to overcome challenges in marriage. If you don't learn to abstain from illegitimate sex before marriage you may not be able to learn how to do so when you get married. It may be too late to learn how to abstain. Apart from learning how to abstain from sex we must also learn how to honour financial obligations and other responsibilities. This is because sex occupies less than 10% of marriage life. Over 90% of the time is spent on managing the home pursuing careers and rendering service to the LORD. Even though sex is part of marriage, we cannot equate sex to marriage. If you have experience in having sex it does not mean you are prepared for marriage.

Indeed you may be over 90% unprepared for marriage.

When you abstain from sex for many years you acquire a very important virtue, PATIENCE!! And you will need a lot of patience in your marriage. All kinds of misunderstanding may arise in marriage which will try your patience, but by then you would have already learnt how to be patient. You may have to wait for long to see your wishes come to pass. If you can abstain (from sex) for 20 years, what can't you wait for?

There are practical analogies which can help solidify your resolve to abstain as the following paragraphs show.

A marriage counsellor once stated that indulging in premarital sex is like stealing what belongs to you, like we see in this example:

Kojo's birthday falls on the 10th of January. On the 1st of January Kwesi decides to present a mobile phone to Kojo as a birthday present. Kojo gets to know that Kwesi desires to give him a birthday present. So Kojo goes to Kwesi's house and secretly picks the mobile phone in question, brings it to his house and begins to use it. Hasn't Kojo stolen what belongs to him? He has! Can't Kojo wait for his birthday to arrive for Kwesi to wrap the present (mobile phone) nicely and make a formal presentation to him? He can! There has to be a formal presentation. During a marriage ceremony, the woman is formally presented to the man and the couple is then formally presented to the witnesses. Sex should not take place before this formal presentation.

Engaging in premarital sex is like playing the opening match before the opening ceremony. There is no world class tournament without an opening ceremony and the opening ceremony precedes all the matches in the tournament. It is weird for the opening match to be played only for the stadium announcer to declare that the opening ceremony will then follow. Marriage is a first class institution set up by GOD. The marriage ceremony should precede the first sexual act. Engaging in premarital sex is just like putting the cart before the horse.

In the sport of athletics, before a race takes place, the starter announces as follows: on your marks..., get set..., (then the gun is fired) and the athletes set off. An individual who indulges in premarital sex is like an athlete who does not allow the sequence to complete. On your marks......... and he is gone!

"He has jumped the gun". It is a false start. Premarital sex is a false start.

A long distance runner who rests adequately in preparation for a 10 kilometre marathon and does not dissipate his energy running about will perform creditably in the marathon.

He has reserved all his energy and has fresh legs. His enthusiasm is very high. However an athlete who takes part in an 800 metre race just before the marathon will perform below his greatest ability. His energy level has dropped greatly and he will begin the marathon with tired legs.

His enthusiasm is low. **Indulging in premarital sex is like taking part in an 800 metre race just before a 10 kilometre marathon.** Marriage is a marathon in various respects including intimacy. In most cases marriage lasts for many years but courtship usually lasts for a few years or for a number of months. So why engage in a short period of intimacy in courtship just before the long period of intimacy in marriage. Why not wait, so that you can begin your marriage with a lot of enthusiasm.

A mother leaves for work early in the morning. She has already prepared her son's lunch. The food, which happens to be the boy's favourite, is giving off a tantalizing aroma. He is tempted, but lunch time is several hours away. His mum will return late in the night. He will have to spend longer hours without food if he eats his lunch in the morning. Lunch time will arrive, he can wait. Your marriage will come to pass, you can wait. Time flies. Your marriage will become a reality sooner than you think. Have faith in GOD, "your time will come."

CHAPTER 6

MORE PRACTICAL REASONS TO ABSTAIN

It is better to enter into marriage with no sexual experience than to enter into marriage with sexual experience. These are the reasons:

If you have no sexual experience (i.e. you are a novice) it means that there is a lot to discover. If there is a lot to discover, it suggests that it will take you a long time or many years of marriage to discover everything. This means that for many years there will be excitement in your marriage. Since the excitement is sustained so long as there is something to discover. When there is nothing more to discover the excitement or the passion dies down. This stage can be described as the **stage of minimum interest.** The interest of the couple at the level of intimacy is low at this point.

Sex can be described as a journey of discovery or exploration. Every journey has got an end. Research shows that, generally speaking, as a marriage grows older, the couple spend less time on sex. This is because they are getting closer to the end of the journey of discovery. There is very little left to discover.

If you know the most about something you are the least excited about it. If you know the least about something, you are the most excited about it. At the stage of minimum interest, the level of expectation is low because they know each other too well. Hence the excitement is also low. Every marriage that lasts will get to this stage. In the Ghanaian society marriage is said to be like the sugarcane. As one chews a piece of sugarcane, it gets to a point when the sugar gets finished and the piece of sugarcane becomes tasteless. This point can be likened to the stage of minimum interest.

At the stage of minimum interest the temptations of adultery are at their peak (the temptations of adultery are ever present even in the early stages of marriage). At this stage some couples do not engage in the act anymore. They have finished discovering each other, "they have seen it all and done it all" (as it is often said).

At the beginning, the passion was so great that they could not keep their hands off each other. They were both crazy about each other in the past. They could not resist each other, now they can't stand each other. Some couples who previously threw their arms around each other in a loving way will now be throwing punches at each other (a typical case of domestic violence). The passion is finished!

In such a case a weak spouse may yield to the temptation of discovering someone else (adultery). Don't rush into sex otherwise you will be rushing to the stage of minimum interest. A couple that had sex before marriage will get to the stage of minimum interest earlier than the couple that abstained till marriage. It is helpful to reach the stage of minimum interest later in marriage when you are more mature or experienced and therefore can handle temptation better (a time when your hormones are not "running wild" and are not being produced in large quantities) It also means that there will be more years of excitement and fewer years of boredom. When you reach the stage of minimum interest early in marriage, it will be more difficult to handle temptation since your hormones will still be running wild and your maturity level will be lower. There will be fewer years of excitement and more years of boredom. Do not begin the journey of discovery before marriage. Start late so that you can end late. It should not be a problem at all, if the two of you are totally green or have no sexual experience at the time you get married. This is because the two of you then become like study mates. The best study mates are those who are at the same or similar level of knowledge or understanding (no one patronizes the other). The two of you discover together. The two of you negotiate the learning curve together. You grow together. After all, married couples are supposed to do things together.

There is a difference between the love two people feel for each other and the passion they feel for each other. The love is the general affection they have and the passion is that strong or intense feeling they have for each other. If a marriage lasts for fifty (50) years, it is possible for the love to last for fifty years; but not the passion. The passion will get finished at a point within the marriage. **At any rate, the passion is not enough for the full length of a long lasting-marriage. The passion is too strong to last for long.** Even the full complement of the passion is not enough. (Since the full complement of the passion is not enough, you make the situation worse by consuming some of the passion before marriage). And so **your marriage desperately needs all the passion you can give to it.** The human body cannot sustain the passion forever. The passion is soon extinguished or burnt out. Even the perpetual flame which is lighted during national celebrations does not burn perpetually. It is soon put out after the celebrations.

We know that no matter the extent to which hot water boils, it will definitely cool when taken off the fire. The passion is a limited or non-renewable resource. If it gets finished, that is it, it's finished!

If you engage in romance, intimacy or sex before marriage you are consuming the already limited passion. You are simply depriving your marriage of the full complement of the passion that it truly deserves. So by the time you finally get married, the passion you have for each other will have reduced significantly or considerably and your marriage will suffer for it. (Instead of entering into marriage with the full complement or 100% of the passion you have for each other, you will be entering with less than the full complement of the passion). You will be beginning your marriage with a serious passion deficiency and thereby hurting your marriage badly. You will then run out of passion early in marriage. Hence the excitement will be lost early. And as many counsellors put it, you will stop enjoying the marriage within a short period of time and start enduring the marriage. The passion that a man and a woman have for each other reduces after each act of intimacy. When you kiss or fondle, it is just like using a tea cup to fetch water from a barrel. The quantity of water in the barrel reduces and thus the water level drops by about 1 millimetre (1mm) or less, but the human eye may not be able to detect this tiny reduction. And you may think the water level has not reduced at all. Similarly when you kiss or caress in the dating or courtship period you may be erroneously thinking that the passion remains intact or no passion is lost. Oh! It's just a kiss. But in actual fact, you are gradually kissing away the passion. These little acts of intimacy should not be taken for granted. "Little drops of water make a mighty ocean" they say. When you engage in sex before marriage it is like using a gallon to fetch water from a barrel. Here, the reduction in the water level is very obvious. So this time around a lot of passion is consumed.

In this case the damage done to your future marriage is even greater. This is why dating or courtship should be strictly platonic. The passion belongs to your marriage not to your courtship. But some partners even consume more of the passion in dating and courtship leaving very little for the marriage. This can be termed as "Aaye fe notsɛ" a popular Ga phrase (literally meaning consuming more than the owner, marriage being the owner in this case). Not even the smallest fraction of the passion should be consumed before marriage. Keep all the passion for your marriage. **You cannot prevent the passion from finishing but you can delay the finishing point of the passion.** When you postpone sex or intimacy till marriage you are delaying the finishing point of the passion, since the passion will endure for the greatest period of time in the marriage before dying out. You must sacrifice your pleasure for your marriage; your marriage is worth that sacrifice. When you abstain from premarital sex, you are investing passion and emotion in your marriage and it is very profitable.

When you engage in sex before marriage, you are investing too much emotion and passion in the dating or courtship. These are risky investments, because dating and courtship will not always end in marriage. The emotional cost of a break up will then be very high. Do yourself a favour by abstaining till marriage.

This illustration buttresses this point sufficiently. Kofi decides to give ¢100.00 to Kwame his friend as a gift (Kwame is in dire need of this money). Kofi then comes across a luxurious item which requires that he uses the ¢100.00 he put aside for Kwame to purchase it. But Kofi says to himself, "I love Kwame so much that I won't even take a pesewa from the ¢100.00.

I will reserve all the money for Kwame. Therefore by extension it is very obvious that **you must love your marriage well enough to reserve all the intimate moments for it.** (This means that premarital sex is out of the question). Reserve all the kisses for your marriage, your marriage deserves it. Regard your marriage as a priceless gift. Give your marriage a VIP treatment. Save the best for it. Do you love your marriage that well, that strongly, that intimately to reserve all the intimate moments for it? Well, that is the question.

If you love something dearly or regard it highly you will sacrifice your personal comfort for it. JESUS CHRIST loved the Church (his bride) so dearly that he sacrificed his life for it and he got his life back. When you forgo pleasure for the sake of your marriage, you will get the pleasure back in marriage and even more. The total reserve of all the passion for your marriage is a well deserved treat for you.

The passion helps you to overcome the problems or frustrations in your marriage. The passion motivates you to keep your marriage. It helps to sustain your interest in the marriage. Certainly there will be problems or challenges in your marriage. You cannot totally avoid them. If the passion is high it will overshadow the problems in your marriage. If the passion is low the problems will overwhelm you. If you enter into marriage with less than 100% of the passion you will **soon** be overwhelmed by the problems in your marriage. Your marriage will then be greatly threatened even in the early stages of the union. The more the passion the better for your marriage.

The passion is akin to a high grade fuel. The marriage runs smoothly on high passion. Again the passion can be likened to a lubricant. The passion lubricates the marriage. Scientifically speaking a lubricant reduces friction in engines (Friction is the force which tends to oppose the relative motion between two bodies in contact). The lubricant ensures that the metal parts rub over each other smoothly. There is less wear and tear. The lubricant helps reduce overheating of the engine. Grammatically speaking, in marriage, the highest passion produces the lowest friction (Friction in this case refers to hostility or quarrelling). In other words **the highest passion produces the lowest tension** (i.e. anger or bitterness). The passion is inversely proportional to the tension. The last thing you want is to enter into marriage with high tension. Such a situation will lead to turbulence in your marriage. You easily see certain flaws about each other that do not exist. When the passion is high you are less critical of each other and you get along easily. There is peace at home. Begin your marriage with the highest passion (100%) to guarantee the lowest tension at the onset of the marriage. The passion is the life-blood for your marriage. It is the oxygen for your marriage. When the oxygen (passion) is low your marriage will be panting for breath; it will be suffocating. The passion is essential to the health of the marriage. The average sleep requirement of the human body is eight (8) hours. The average passion requirement of marriage is a hundred percent. No marriage requires less than 100% of the passion.

If you are embarking on a journey covering hundreds of kilometres (like a journey from Accra to Tamale), you will need a full tank of fuel to be on the safe side. Even if the fuel is not enough, you will run out of fuel close to your destination; a walking distance away. You can then practically and comfortably walk to your destination. If you however embark on a jolly ride within the suburbs of Accra (i.e. premarital sex) before the actual journey from Accra to Tamale begins, you will be starting your journey with less than a full tank of fuel. This time around you will run out of fuel at a point that is very far from the destination.

You will now have to walk laboriously to your destination. This will drain your energy and you will be extremely tired. Worse still, you may end up abandoning or terminating the journey (i.e. divorce). Save all the fuel for your marriage. It is a wise choice.

The following narrative provides yet another good reason to abstain from premarital sex.

A young man and a young woman are madly in love with each other (they are head over heels in love). The two of them are experiencing Hot-Blooded Passion. The temptation to fornicate is so high, yet they resist. Their hormones are running wild, yet they resist. Their bodies are craving, yet they resist. Feeling no ye deep, yet they resist. The years of abstinence from sex produce a lot of stress. Now, when you apply stress or pressure to a system, there is usually a temperature increase. Therefore the Hot Blooded Passion becomes hotter. Indeed, Red Hot (on account of the massive accumulation of the stress of abstinence). Meanwhile they are still abstaining; they are still keeping their feelings in check. They are so determined not to consume any of the passion before marriage.

After a few years of courtship and following many years of abstinence, they finally get married. They have won the battle of abstinence. They have finished serving the ban.

Now the ban has been lifted. The barrier has been broken, and they are now totally free.

And then they let go or unleash the Very Hot-Blooded Passion that was so restricted or bottled up under pressure. Now what do you think is going to happen? There is going to be an explosion of passion!

The explosion of passion is simply a sensation beyond description. It is an overwhelming experience. For those choosing abstinence, this is what you are bargaining for. This is definitely a better deal.

We can derive this simple formula from this scenario: **Hot Blooded Passion + Stress or Pressure = Explosion of Passion.** When a balloon is filled with air, the air exerts pressure on the walls of the balloon. When the neck of the balloon is opened the air escapes with speed and the balloon moves about in random motion. This is like the explosion of passion. The pressure that builds up in a bottle of champagne produces a popping sound when it is opened. It is also like the explosion of passion. The explosion of passion will have a positive and a lasting impact on you. Do not deny yourself the explosion of passion.

You deserve it. It must be noted that it is the tremendous build up of pressure or the great accumulation of stress that leads to the explosion of passion. Stress is that important ingredient that produces the explosion of passion. Without stress there is no explosion of passion. And this stress is provided by kind courtesy of abstinence. People who indulge in premarital sex miss the explosion of passion because they don't accumulate massive stress. The little stress that develops is relieved by engaging in premarital sex.

An individual who totally abstains for 20 years (from puberty to adulthood) accumulates massive stress. This massive stress will definitely produce a massive explosion of passion when it is finally released in marriage. The prospect of a massive explosion of passion is enough motivation for an individual to abstain till marriage. A prospective couple who completely abstain, look forward to the explosion of passion with pleasure.

The ban on sex is the price you pay for the explosion of passion. It is not too high a price to pay. The human body has been created by GOD to cope with many kinds of stress, including the stress of abstinence.

"The accumulated stress, when released at the appropriate time, produces desirable results. If you have chosen to abstain before marriage, keep on accumulating the stress.

Many people complain that abstinence is not a convenient option to take. Their excuse? Abstinence is stressful.

Abstinence is palpably stressful. But stress can produce excitement, as clearly shown in the narrative, a few paragraphs above. Other everyday examples also confirm this fact.

"Thank GOD it's Friday" is a popular saying which is well known among the working class in general. A lot of stress is accumulated throughout the working week by waking up very early in the morning, rushing to work to avoid being late, working speedily to beat deadlines and spending hours in heavy traffic. When Friday arrives, many a worker becomes excited because there is a restful weekend close by. However, if you are at home on holiday, vacation or leave, Friday becomes less special to you, since the stress is very low or non-existent.

An expectant mother undergoes a lot of stress during the period of pregnancy. Within the 9 month period she may experience morning sickness (involving nausea and vomiting), swelling of the feet and unusual food cravings. Finally she goes through a painful process of labour. After childbirth she is overjoyed because all the stress is gone and she has a new baby.

Students study hard at school for many years and sometimes have to contend with bullying and other challenges. When they finally graduate after strenuous examinations they experience an outburst of excitement, because the stress is all gone.

A gentleman walks along the street and then he feels the urge to urinate. But there is no suitable place close by to enable him relieve himself. The nearest urinal is a kilometre away.

He experiences a lot of discomfort, the stress is immense but he is simply committed to doing the right thing.

He is waiting for the right place and the right time to let go! That is the principle, **The Right Place And The Right Time To Let Go**. It is all about timing.

Eccl 3:1-8 tells us that there is time for everything. If the timing is right, what you are doing is right. If the timing is wrong, what you are doing is wrong. Premarital sex is wrong because the timing is wrong. We must get the timing right! The timing must be spot on! It is about precision timing.

Now when the man gets to the urinal and finally lets go he experiences great relief.

We can compare the stress the man went through to the stress of abstinence. The discomfort in both cases yield pleasure in the end. The man had remarkable control over his bladder. The individual who abstains has exceptional control over the sexual urge.

People who abstain from sex till marriage have the best of the world of abstinence and the best of the world of indulgence. They make the most of their marriages.

1. They have the best of the world of abstinence because they end up becoming graduates of abstinence (i.e. They achieve mastery of the art of abstinence which is critical for the survival of any marriage)

2. They have the best of the world of indulgence because they experience the explosion of passion. And it comes with a clear conscience. They truly let go. (They have valuable experience in abstaining from the act and in engaging in the act. Those who chose not to abstain have experience only in engaging in the act).

Ama feels thirsty for five (5) minutes and she drinks a cup of water. Yaa feels thirsty for five (5) hours and she also drinks a cup of water. Which of the two ladies will enjoy the cup of water better? The answer is more than obvious.

Yaa will enjoy the cup of water better because Yaa underwent more stress. If you feel thirsty for 10 hours before quenching your thirst, that cup of water will be memorable. You may end up dreaming about that cup of water that very night. Food tastes better after a long fast. A person who works for ten(10) years in order to buy a car will be far more excited about his car than a person who works for only one year to buy a car. The lesson we can draw from these examples is simply this "**The longer the period of denial the higher the level of sensation**" When the human body is longing for pleasure and that pleasure is kept away from the body for a long time, the body enjoys that pleasure better when it finally receives it. If you are tired of abstaining from sex for years remember this lesson.

Kofi has never been to prison before. He has been free all his life (like those who do not abstain). Kwame has been serving a ten

(10) year prison term with hard labour and he is due for release. He has been enduring a punishing schedule by digging trenches and carrying heavy loads. He longs to be free (he is so passionate about freedom). He is then released from prison. Initially, he can't believe he is free. He thinks he is dreaming. His excitement is beyond description. A day after his release from prison he wakes up to the fact that he is truly free (the reality sinks down). As one will put it, the prisoner feels as though a great weight has been lifted from him. And he feels light. Everyday of freedom is like a day in paradise for him. When you eventually get married after years of abstinence, you feel the same way as a prisoner who has just been released from prison. Freedom then becomes very special to you. A man who has been free all his life does not see freedom as particularly special. He did not struggle for his freedom. Freedom came easily for him. He may even fail to notice that he is free because his problems easily overshadow his freedom. But for a man who has just been released from prison, his freedom overshadows all his problems. The mere fact that he can move about freely is exciting enough for him.

If you are abstaining from sex, admittedly you are a prisoner of a kind. But thank GOD you are not in a prison with iron bars. You are free to pursue your dreams, move about and go about your daily activities unhindered. You are only serving a ban on sex (not serving a prison term). When you ultimately get into marital union, the mere fact that the ban on sex has been lifted will be exciting enough for you.

The ex-prisoner understands freedom better, cherishes freedom better, enjoys freedom better and is more likely to treat freedom with the respect it deserves (he is less likely to take freedom for granted). The person who abstains till marriage understands intimacy better, cherishes intimacy better, enjoys intimacy better and is more likely to treat sex with the respect it deserves (he is less likely to take sex for granted). He doesn't consider sex to be ordinary but special.

A survey was once conducted to find out from people what true happiness is. It was revealed that people appreciate true happiness better, if they experienced true sadness in the past. There is a huge gap between true sadness and true happiness. True sadness is at the bottom of the ladder and true happiness is at the top. So when you move from true sadness to true happiness the elevation is very great. Hence making you experience happiness at its greatest extent. The ex-prisoner enjoys freedom better than the man who has always been free because the ex-prisoner compares his present state of freedom (i.e. True happiness) to his years of hardship in prison (i.e. true sadness) and notices the great difference between the two and thus becomes very grateful to GOD. In the same way those who abstained till they got married enjoy intimacy better than those who indulged in sex before marriage because they compare the freedom they now have to express themselves sexually (i.e. true happiness) to the many years they starved themselves of intimacy (i.e. true sadness) and they notice the great difference between the two periods and they become thankful to GOD for obtaining their freedom.

When you experience a lot of difficulties or strain before laying hands on something you passionately desire, you appreciate it more.

So the initial strain of abstinence before marriage gives you enough reason to be grateful for intimacy in marriage. And you complain less about your marriage. As it is sufficiently known, "easy come, easy go". The axiom "you don't know what you have till you lose it" supports this argument. It is also true that you value what you have better if you were initially deprived of it. People who initially deprived themselves of intimacy till marriage know the true value of intimacy because it did not come easily.

The Ghanaian youth of today are not so excited about the independence of Ghana. The reason is simple. They have never experienced the oppression of colonial authority before. They don't know how it feels like to be deprived of their freedom.

There is nothing to which they can compare their freedom. They can't compare and contrast. If your courtship is strictly platonic, sex, intimacy or romance become the differences between your courtship and your marriage. In this case, there is a sharp contrast between your courtship and your marriage and hence it provides a very strong basis for comparing and contrasting. **The greater the difference between your marriage and your courtship, the more excited you will be about your marriage.** Therefore it is in your own interest, to deliberately create as many differences as possible between your marriage and your courtship in favour of your marriage. So that when you do get married you can appreciate the difference. An artist creates a piece of art work so that he can appreciate it. Aside from the money he can make from selling that piece of artwork.

Therefore create a difference, so that you can appreciate the difference. If a painter does not create any painting, there will be nothing to appreciate.

If you don't create any difference between your marriage and your courtship there will be no difference to appreciate in marriage. You may decide not to kiss whiles dating or courting, that is one difference. You may also decide not to fondle before marriage, that is another difference. Think of the other differences. If you can create ten differences, go ahead! You can then appreciate all those (ten) differences in addition to the other benefits of marriage.

People who indulged in premarital sex before entering into marriage do not experience any change as far as the way they interact with each other or relate to each other at the physical level is concerned. What they do in marriage is the same as what they used to do in courtship.

People who indulge in premarital sex are duplicating marriage. They push dating or courtship to the same level as marriage. In this case, the passage from courtship to marriage becomes a mere horizontal movement. An ordinary shift from left to right.

When people abstain while courting, they put courtship in its proper position; meaning that they place courtship far below the level of marriage. So there is a huge difference between the two. When they get married, they move the relationship to a higher level. They move it to a higher gear.

The passage from courtship to marriage then becomes a significant vertical movement. A giant leap! (from bottom to top). Which one do you prefer? The ordinary shift or the giant leap? Relatively speaking, the ordinary shift is boring, the giant leap is exciting. The difference is clear!

When you abstain while you are courting, you introduce a lot of suspense into the "equation"; the suspense of the unknown (since you don't know each other as far as intimacy is concerned). And the suspense of the unknown can be very thrilling. If you are abstaining in your relationship, enjoy the suspense. It is said that "the thrill is in the chase," When a man expresses interest in a woman, he is not sure whether she will accept his proposal or not (that is the suspense of the unknown). It is thrilling and makes him go all out to win her heart.

Everybody wants the excitement in his or her marriage to last for as long as possible. To ensure this, one must enter into marriage with the highest possible level of excitement. This is because the highest possible level of excitement will last for the longest possible period of time. Now, having established this fact, the question then arises, "how do you enter into marriage with the highest possible level of excitement?" You can only enter into marriage with the highest possible level of excitement by abstaining from intimacy or sex before marriage.

There should be no sexual contact of any kind. This guarantees that all the levels of intimacy become totally new to you in marriage. A famous quote reveals that when a man opens the door of his car for his wife, either the car is new or the wife is new (or perhaps both are new). When a new year arrives, many people make new year resolutions but as the year grows older, most people abandon their resolutions. Things that are new generate excitement. Therefore total newness generates total excitement.

If intimacy is totally new to you in marriage, you will be totally excited about intimacy in marriage. You achieve your fullest excitement potential. We must aspire to enter into marriage with total newness, because that is the only way we will be totally excited about our marriages. Total virgins enter into marriage with total newness. Total newness means high expectations. Expectations are high because there is a "mystery" to unravel; there is something to find out. At the time when a couple who are total virgins get married, the love is great, the passion is high, the excitement is high, the suspense is high, the enthusiasm is high, expectations are high, "bibiara da high." They start their marriage on a high note; they start from the peak of excitement. Entering into marriage as a virgin is not the old-fashioned way, it is the smart way! People who indulge in sex before marriage enter into marriage with partial excitement (which is far below the peak of excitement, because the peak occurs before the marriage). The peak of excitement must occur within the marriage and not before it. We must reach the peak at the right time. When you defer sex till marriage you are only raising the level of excitement to be experienced in marriage.

Familiarity they say breeds contempt but absence makes the heart grow fonder. When a man and a woman indulge in premarital sex, they obtain carnal knowledge of each other hence they become familiar with each other; predictably they enter into marriage with a significant level of contempt. However for the prospective couple that chooses to abstain, the absence of intimacy or sex in courtship makes them fonder of each other. They enter into marriage with little or no contempt because they do not know each other carnally, yet.

A story is told of a man and a woman who had sex with each other while they were courting. They then got married and went for their honeymoon. During the honeymoon, the man was busy working on the computer and attending to other business. He did not pay attention to his wife, there was no romance. His wife was visibly shocked. So she asked her husband, "why are you not paying attention to me; why are you not touching me?" We are on our honeymoon for goodness sake! Then the man said, Ah! But what is new?

If they abstained from sex during courtship, he would not have behaved the way he did on their honeymoon. Some people are of the view that courtship is more enjoyable than marriage. If you abstain during courtship you will not make this argument.

A great deal of excitement is associated with doing something for the first time. I prefer to call this "**THE FIRST TIME EUPHORIA**". If you wear a brand new shoe for the first time, you walk as if you are modelling, you walk with calculated steps. You try hard to avoid scratches on your shoe. It is the first time euphoria! But after wearing the same shoe for the second time and a number of times after that, the newness is lost and you may even kick a stone with it. When a person visits a tourist site for the first time, he or she is extremely excited about the place. On the second visit however the excitement level about the place drops.

During a typical wedding ceremony, (after the exchange of vows and the unveiling of the bride), the officiating minister declares, "you may kiss the bride" and then the groom proceeds to kiss the bride. Now I can assure you that this statement, "you may kiss the bride" will mean a great deal to you, if that kiss happens to be the very first kiss!

The first time euphoria is one of the best experiences you can have. Keep the first time euphoria for your marriage.

If your first ever sexual encounter takes place in marriage, the first time euphoria will occur in marriage.

The first time euphoria will then form part of the history of the marriage. If after many years, you decide to evaluate your marriage, the first time euphoria will then be one of the high points of the marriage.

You will never forget the first time you engage in the sexual act.

Now, if you will never forget it, then it better be associated with a clear conscience and with fulfilment. It should put a smile and not a frown on your face any time you remember it.

If your first sexual encounter is premarital sex, then it will be associated with guilt or regret, which is unfortunate. In some cases, it will be associated with doubt and bitterness.

In such circumstances, the first sexual encounter will put a frown on your face as frequently as you remember it. You can avoid this mental torture by abstaining till marriage. The person with whom you break your virginity will often occupy your thoughts. Let that person be your husband or wife. Let no one else compete with your spouse to be the occupier of your thoughts. The first sexual act will determine your perception or impression about sex. It is said that "there is never a second chance for a first impression." The first sexual act will have a huge impact on you so wait for the right time (which is in marriage).

CHAPTER 7

THE LONG TERM COMPLICATIONS OF
PREMARITAL SEX

Any advantage of premarital sex is an advantage with a baggage (an advantage with a serious side effect).

You don't need an advantage with a baggage. There are no justifiable advantages of premarital sex. If you should put the advantages and disadvantages of premarital sex on a scale, the scale will tilt in favour of the disadvantages. The overall effect or the net effect of premarital sex is negative.

When a person sleeps with twenty (20) people, all of them obtain carnal knowledge of him or her and there is a lot they can do with that knowledge. Some people keep records of the people they sleep with. They write down every detail of their sexual experiences.

They put down such sensitive information in "log books" which are otherwise known as slum books. These slum books contain the wildest and most scandalous details one can think of.

If you decide to "sort yourself out" by sleeping with someone you are not married to (on just one occasion) you may end up getting your details in a slum book. In today's world where a lot of people misuse technology, you could be recorded on video and pictures could be taken of you. When they leak, you would be greatly embarrassed and your reputation would be seriously damaged.

A clear example of short-term pleasure leading to long-term consequences. When you sleep with someone, you certainly lose your privacy to that person and you lose a part of you to him or her. Whiles you are engrossed in the sexual act, you are vulnerable. Anything harmful can be done to you in the heat of the moment.

A lot of playboys abound these days, and they keep on looking for victims. They have an ungodly ambition of sleeping with as many women as possible. Any woman who has an affair with a playboy is helping him to achieve his aim. A playboy has a whole set of women of various backgrounds of whom he has taken advantage (some of them may be "ladies of the night"). And he goes about bragging about it. He uses the women to boost his ego and to "enhance his profile", just like a fighter enhances his profile with every person he defeats. A playboy considers each woman he sleeps with as an object of his conquest. To him, she is just a statistical unit (just adding up to the numbers). A woman who indulges in premarital sex risks being disrespected by a playboy. He will just add her to his long unenviable list. One cannot tell who is a playboy and who is not by simply looking at them.

According to William Shakespeare, there is no art to find the mind's construction in the face. Many men have also had their lives messed up just because they allowed their sexual feelings to get the better part of them.

We cannot play down the long-term psychological effect of premarital sex. When you genuinely repent of the sin of premarital sex, GOD forgives you. Unfortunately some people are not able to forgive themselves. It has been often quoted that "GOD forgives us more than we forgive ourselves". Even if you are able to forgive yourself, you may not be able to lose that regrettable memory. Your brain literally decides on its own which experiences to store and which ones not to store. We can confirm the fact that there are times when remembering what you said or did on a particular day becomes difficult and even impossible. There are also instances when a person cannot forget a particular bad experience no matter how hard he or she tries.

Sexual encounters are examples of experiences that are extremely difficult to forget (as stated in the previous chapter). You will be having flashbacks of those encounters even when you are married. The memories may haunt you or eat you up.

You will not be proud of your past; and you will be wondering why you yielded.

If you are able to abstain throughout your single life you can freely discuss your past with your husband or wife. Your spouse's trust in you will be very solid. You will have nothing to hide. You will not be struggling to keep any secret for fear of a backlash from your spouse. Edgar Watson Howe once said that, "A man who can keep secrets is wise, but he is half as wise as a man who has no secrets to keep". Why struggle to keep a secret when you have the option of not having that secret in the first place?

The complications of premarital sex can easily be avoided if one resolves to abstain. If you do a "cost-benefit" analysis you will realize that you are better off abstaining till marriage.

CHAPTER 8

CONCLUSION

Premarital sex can never qualify as a curtain raiser to marriage. A person who insists on premarital sex may lose a good future husband or wife who does not believe in sex before marriage.

Having sex before marriage does not guarantee that you will make the right choice of a life partner. You may fail to assess the qualities of the person properly. The focus on sex can cloud your judgement.

If you conduct a solid background check on the person you intend to marry, you will be able to determine whether he or she will make a suitable partner. Cohabitation is definitely not an option to choose. Proponents of this kind of relationship claim that it will help you to know your partner better during courtship. However a person can successfully hide his or her true character until you marry him or her. The eagerness to marry may be lost, since you are already living together as a married couple does. Also, it is very easy to yield to the temptation of having sex before marriage. Many cultures frown on sex before marriage. In the Ghanaian society, when pregnancy occurs before marriage the man responsible for the pregnancy is usually asked to pay a penalty. Many religions including Christianity do not support premarital sex. Bible quotations like Eph. 5:3, Acts 15:20, 1 Cor. 6:13 and 1 Thess. 4:3, speak emphatically against premarital sex.

Abstinence from premarital sex is a cultural and religious issue just as it is a logical issue.

Take the liberty of saying no to premarital sex. You have the power of choice or the power to choose. Choose abstinence, it yields "dividends" in marriage.

www.ingramcontent.com/pod-product-compliance
Lightning Source LLC
Chambersburg PA
CBHW072036060426
42449CB00010BA/2292